The Way We Were

The British on Holiday

The Way We Were

The British on Holiday

TIM GLYNNE-JONES

ARCTURUS

ARCTURUS

This edition published in 2016 by
Arcturus Publishing Limited
26/27 Bickels Yard, 151–153 Bermondsey Street,
London SE1 3HA

Copyright © Arcturus Holdings Limited

ISBN: 978-1-78428-298-1
AD005268UK

Cover design: Maki Ryan

Printed in China

Contents

· ·

Introduction

....

As a nation surrounded by water, it's hardly surprising that the British have always jumped at the chance of a sojourn by the seaside. For most of the population that chance only arose with the Industrial Revolution and the spreading tentacles of the railways to coastal towns like Blackpool, Scarborough and Weston-super-Mare. By the start of the 20th century, the invigorating benefits of a paddle in the briny were well known to much of the population who would leave the cities in organized packs for their annual fix of fresh air. The song *I Do Like To Be Beside The Seaside* was written in 1907.

The First World War changed many aspects of British life, including the way we took holidays. An increasing focus on leisure time and the pursuit

of happiness prompted visionary businessmen like Billy Butlin to shape the holiday resort in a way that catered precisely for the growing wave of fun-hungry holidaymakers. The seaside was a place where you could let your hair down, dance and jump around without causing public outrage.

The Second World War put a brake on the expansion of the holiday industry, but it returned with a vengeance in peacetime. The bounds of holiday travel soon extended beyond our shores to the Côte d'Azur, Costa Blanca and even to other continents, as the British took the concept of the seaside resort around the world. Throughout this evolution in holiday habits, there was always a photographer on hand. The pictures they captured provide a fascinating and nostalgic record of those wonderful happy times.

There is a timeless quality to the image of children playing in the sea. Their behaviour, their attire and the sea itself are consistent with any period in history. Stripped down, simple pleasures abound at the seaside and the British embraced this truth wholeheartedly in the 19th century – surprising perhaps, given the unreliability of British holiday season weather and the temperature of the sea that laps at this sceptered isle.

Wish You Were Here

But the British love of the beach was born out of a desire for stimulation, not lukewarm luxury, and by the interwar years there was plenty of invigoration to be found beside the seaside. The 1920s marked an age when the beach became a recreation ground where the postwar thirst for fun and frolics could be quenched in a state of undress that would have been frowned upon anywhere else.

The railways had opened up resorts like Blackpool and Morecambe to the masses, and now the motor car and charabanc were making new holiday destinations even more accessible to even more people. The outdoor life, fitness and sun worship were de rigueur and the British took their holidays in search of all three, wherever they managed to get to.

If you can't get to the water, let the water come to you. A group of children in Windsor are delighted to find their local park has been transformed into a swimming lake as a result of the River Thames bursting its banks during the summer holidays.

*Any day out from the usual daily routine was a day to be cherished.
Laughter and hijinx were the order of the day. On a warm summer's day
in 1922 a group of children of various ages gather at the walls of Bishop's
Park in Fulham ready to go off on an excursion.*

A picnic outing to Kennack Sands in Cornwall around the turn of the century shows that our ancestors enjoyed a spot of fresh air and a scenic view just as much as we do today. No one's wearing a swimming cossie though. Those hats, jackets and ankle-length skirts remain firmly in place.

Left *A trip to the beach was an opportunity for young women to enjoy the thrill of sartorial liberation. Bare legs and arms were acceptable on the beach, as demonstrated by these two bathing beauties, modelling the classic one-piece bathing costume of the 1920s, and soon they'd be cutting it on the dance floor too.*

Above *With their faithful hound leading the way and a deckchair between them carrying everything that was needed for a day by the sea, two men wend their way homewards after long hours of sunshine somewhere in the south of England. Next stop, the pub…*

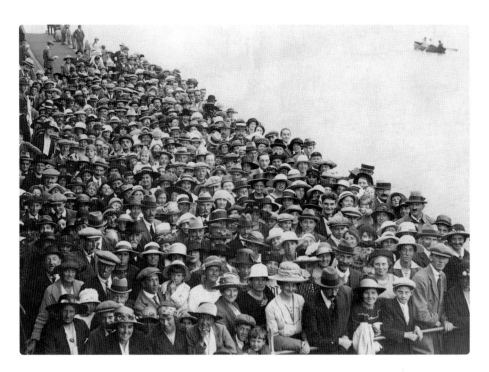

Despite the crush, these 1920s trippers waiting to catch a boat ride from Bournemouth Pier are in high spirits, encouraged no doubt by the presence of the camera. Without cameras of their own, images of summer holiday excursions had to be stored in the memory.

The British fairground 'galloper' was a merry-go-round featuring wooden horses that went gently up and down as the roundabout turned. Here, you see a group of young women having the time of their lives at a funfair in Wembley on a warm bank holiday back in 1924. You can almost hear the music playing. In the UK, roundabouts mostly spin clockwise, but in Europe and the US they go the other way.

Once again the presence of the camera has all eyes focused in the same direction. As spectators roast on the rocks in hats, jackets and long skirts, a school of beaming bathers cool off in the refreshing waters of Plymouth in 1925.

Above *British beach donkeys are now protected by their own special code – no one over 8 stone can ride them, for example – but in the old days they were a law unto themselves. Here, Barney and Archibald are fed scraps by a stallholder in Ramsgate as they wait for the tide to go out so that rides can begin again.*

Right *For all but the very well off, travelling to the seaside in the 1920s mostly meant taking the train. Two girls in their best going-away attire keep themselves distracted as they wait at Euston Station to be loaded aboard a train bound for summer holiday heaven.*

Left *Bucket, spade, umbrella – some things never change. The essential accoutrements of a holiday by the sea are all needed as this group of children try to squeeze under their mother's brolly to avoid a rogue rain cloud. 'Will it set in?' 'No, it's just a passing shower.'*

Above *A mixed piggy-back race at Shanklin on the Isle of Wight sees runners and riders in high spirits, not to mention the spectators. On the beach, dozens of gleaming white changing tents mark the spot where these revellers transformed from respectable 1920s socialites into naughty children again.*

Say cheese

Children and adults smile for a beach photographer in Clacton-on-Sea. Commercial beach photographers had been plying their trade in Britain's coastal resorts since the 1850s, but the 1920s saw a significant change in the way they went about their work. The collodion positive process they had used up until now to produce one-off portraits 'while you wait' was replaced by the reflex camera. This revolutionary new device enabled the photographers to move around shooting a multitude of subjects. They would then spend their evening developing the prints, which they would display the following day for their subjects to come back and buy.

It was hugely popular and business boomed. The beach photographer himself also developed, from a rather shabby character to a smart, personable professional, adept at putting his subjects at ease. The style of photography changed too. Gone were stiff posed portraits; in came relaxed shots of people having fun.

Holidaymakers promenade up and down Clacton pier in bright sunshine.
The 50-year-old pier was sold into private ownership in the early 1920s
and numerous developments followed aimed at attracting customers and
keeping them there. They included a theatre, a casino and a dance hall.

Parasols and crinoline abound as spectators in punts and rowing boats crowd against the boom separating them from the racing channel at Henley. The Royal Regatta has been drawing the upper echelons of society since 1839 and is still an established fixture in the British 'summer season'.

A group of young hopefuls take their partners
by the hand for an impromptu dance on a
camping trip to Box Hill in Surrey, 1930. The
inter-war years brought a keen interest in
healthy living and, for the first time, camping
became a popular leisure activity.

Right Guests at Tolland Hotel in Bournemouth
take tea in the Solarium, where sand on the
floor and sunray lamps created the effect of
the beach in full sun 24 hours a day. Ultraviolet
light from the sun or sunlamps was strongly
promoted for health benefits.

Dance yourself fitter

Margaret Morris, born in 1891, was a pioneer of movement as a therapeutic exercise. Having established herself as a distinguished dancer and choreographer with her own technique inspired by Isadora Duncan and the Greek school of calisthenics, she set up a club in Chelsea for productions of original works and free discussion. Much of that discussion centred on the health-giving benefits of movement.

Her summer schools helped to establish the concept of a holiday with a purpose. Guests would be educated in the remedial qualities of physical movement and then spend their holiday learning techniques.

Medics, educators and the public bought into Morris' ideas linking movement and aesthetics with physical wellbeing and Margaret Morris Movement spread around the world, while she continued to develop her dance schools. In this picture from 1930, four dancers practise their moves on the beach at Weston-super-Mare.

A group of children with buckets, spades and rubber rings on the sea wall at Birchington in Kent. The inflatable swimming aid had progressed from a car tyre inner tube to a purpose-made ring in bright colours and, in some cases (third from left) animal features for added encouragement.

The freedom of the open road held an irresistible allure for anyone lucky enough to have their own transport. All you had to do was load up with camping gear and golf clubs, wrap up in something warm, don a sensible hat, stick the dog on the front and the world was your oyster. Hang health & safety!

In at the shallow end. A swimming instructor begins with the basics as a class of delighted children prepares to take the plunge while on holiday in Brighton. Learning to swim became part of the school curriculum in 1907 and parents became more aware of the importance of keeping their children safe in the water.

A man selling oysters, whelks and shrimps from a stall on the beach in the early 1930s. Seafood was traditionally working-class fodder, dredged up from the seabed in vast quantities and dished up ready to eat with pepper and vinegar. But the supply of native oysters was in decline and it wouldn't be long before they were regarded as a delicacy for the rich.

Right They're under starter's orders in the Margate donkey derby, while a line-up of charabancs await the word to go at the coach station in the background. Donkeys, sometimes dozens of them, were a familiar feature in British seaside resorts, having originally been used by local fishermen to carry their catch.

You made your own fun in those days. Well, you could if there were enough of you. Here, a crowd of 850 holidaymakers at Caister holiday camp in Norfolk await their turn on the blanket. Caister was one of Britain's first holiday parks when it opened in 1906.

Veterans of a long-forgotten war pull together as they enjoy the beneficial effects of dipping their toes in the briny at Littlehampton. As long as you could roll your trousers up above the knee, that was enough. There was simply no need to remove your jacket or tie.

'Oi, you can't park that thing here.' A group of day-trippers are caught on camera as they try to push a car out of the waves back to shore in 1933. How did the vehicle get there? Since no one seems at all upset you can probably assume it isn't theirs.

A group of schoolchildren look uncertain as to whether they should be smiling or cowering in fear as they are 'entertained' by a ventriloquist and his dummy on the beach at Porthcawl. Children's holiday entertainment often had a rather sinister side to it.

*Despite the signs on the bus, this group of children are not on
their way to Devon but to Epsom Downs. The day out has been
organized by the Society of Friends, in conjunction with the League
of Coloured People and the Coloured Men's Institute, to give
underprivileged London children a taste of the countryside.*

All the nice girls love a sailor, especially if he's offering a smoke.
The pulling power of cigarettes, as it was in the 1930s, is vividly
demonstrated by two Navy men from the destroyer HMS Fury, as they
befriend two bathing beauties during a layover in Jersey.

Glamour at the lido. You didn't have to go to the seaside to enjoy a bathe in the warm sunshine. Open air swimming pools became inundated with water lovers when the sun came out, and the girls could show off their snazzy new two-piece knitted swimsuits.

Right *'Smile! It'll all be over in a minute.' Two lucky winners of a beautiful baby competition on the Isle of Wight are treated to a photo with 'Uncle Arthur', who is desperately trying to live up to his claim to be 'the ugliest man on Sandown Pier'.*

Elderly holidaymakers in Eastbourne observe the time-honoured tradition of sitting in deckchairs and gazing at the horizon. With the prom, the beach and the ever-moving sea in front of them, there was always something to hold their interest until it was time to return to the guest house for tea.

*Snake charmers entertain holidaymakers at Morecambe in Lancashire, 1932.
Snake charming has always been a bit of a racket, where snakes sway in line with
the movements of the flute not because they can hear its music – they can't – but
because they feel threatened. The musician always sits out of range of the cobra's
strike and some snakes had their fangs removed or even their mouths sewn up.*

The Ski Club of Great Britain, which had formed in 1903,
started running ski tours for British holidaymakers in
the 1930s, as the sport began to gain popularity. These
pupils at an indoor ski school in London are learning how
to jump before taking to the slopes.

A group of young men gather round the piano for a sing-song at the Harling Summer Camp. Unemployment was a serious problem in the 1930s and camps like these were organized by the Ministry of Labour in order to give unemployed men work in a holiday atmosphere.

Six young boys peer into the viewing glasses of a row of mutascopes, or 'What the Butler Saw' machines. These risqué machines were very popular seaside attractions. For the price of one penny, you could watch a series of flip cards create the impression of a moving image of a scantily clad girl.

At a glance, it's hard to tell where the beach ends and the sea begins as children, adults and dogs enjoy a hot August day paddling in the shallows. Crowded beaches, like this one at Canvey Island, became a feature of the summer holidays in 1930s Britain.

The spirit of invention was alive and well. If you couldn't afford to buy or hire a boat, you made one. These boys have made good use of some old packing crates and are waiting for the wind to catch their makeshift sail and carry them out to deeper water.

Above *The railway companies didn't just take people to the seaside, they put them up there too, in redundant railway carriages converted into holiday homes. A typical camping coach contained a bedroom, bathroom, kitchen and living room. These campers in 1936 are listening to a gramophone on the 'roof terrace'.*

Looking tanned and gorgeous, a group of friends pose for a snapshot during a holiday on Hayling Island in Hampshire. By the 1930s the British were warming to bare, tanned skin, having not so long before regarded it as a mark of the weather-beaten lower classes.

In the picture

· ·

A man poses as Popeye while his two female companions assume the role of exotic beauties for a seaside photographer with his cheeky cut-out board in Brighton in 1939. With the country on the brink of war, comical cut-out boards helped to keep the people smiling and highlighted a growing appetite for enjoying the good times while they still could.

Seaside photos like these were all about having a laugh and documenting shared enjoyment; they also predated the days when friends crammed into photo-booths or sent one another 'selfies' on phones

Interestingly, the bikini, as worn by the two female characters in the drawing, would not be formally introduced to beach fashion until 1946, when French designer Louis Réard unveiled his skimpy 'invention' to widespread moral outrage.

In a rather bizarre display of British eccentricity, a businessman in full office attire – obviously not one for sunbathing – takes a break from playing with his beach ball to read about the gathering storm in Europe, while everyone else around him catches 40 winks.

Right In a scene reminiscent of the early attempts to fly, a stuntman entertains the crowds on Brighton beach by riding his bike off a diving board. From this angle it looks like he's going to plummet on to the concrete, but he got his angles right and made it into the sea.

Sand crafted

Children look on in awe as an artist puts the finishing touches to a sculpture of a lion killing a serpent in the sand of Teignmouth beach. Some of the children have their own spades and, no doubt, their own ambitions to create fantastical sand structures of their own.

The concept of building sandcastles, vainly fortified against the lapping waves, had been pursued by beach goers ever since the seaside became a popular holiday destination. Sand sculptors had taken the art to a new level in the 19th century and could often earn money from passers-by throwing coins from the promenade while they worked on the sand below.

For children, the tin bucket and wooden-handled spade were holiday essentials if staying by a sandy beach and sandcastle-building competitions were a common feature of the seaside holiday. If you didn't have the artistry, you could always just bury Mum or Dad up to their necks while they were sleeping.

Too much sun will do that to you. The woman on the left looks less than happy about being the bookend for her sleeping companions on Blackpool's sea front in 1939. These days, you might expect people to be more lightly dressed for a soporific summer's day by the seaside, but the standards of the time demanded a thicker cut of cloth.

A year before her death, music hall star Florrie Ford (third from right) joins a somewhat bawdy-looking chorus line making a splash in the sea at Morecambe. Like Ford herself, the Lancashire resort was hugely popular, especially attracting holidaymakers from Yorkshire and Scotland.

Dancing couples in Skegness discover the delights of a whole new holiday concept: the Butlin's Holiday Camp. Billy Butlin opened his first camp in Skegness in 1936 and it proved an instant hit, going on to become one of the most popular destinations for British holidaymakers of all ages.

Getting Away From It All

The oppression of the Second World War put a premium on holidays. Many of the developments in the holiday industry that had begun to evolve in the 1930s were put on hold during wartime and the options for getting away from it all became few and far between. Seaside resorts became front line towns, fortified against possible invasion and certainly not conducive to beachcombing; the new holiday camps closed down and were requisitioned by the Armed Forces; and rationing restricted the availability of many of life's little luxuries.

The British became adept at taking their pleasures where they could and appreciating life's small concessions. For children living with the daily threat of Nazi bombing raids, any time spent away from the city was a relief to be cherished and dreamed about on the train journey home.

When the war ended and the barbed wire, tank traps and unexploded bombs were cleared away, people flocked back to the seaside in huge numbers. But resorts had to change as boarding houses lost popularity and holidaymakers began to prefer bed and breakfasts or campsites to more regimented accommodation. The main thing, however, was that they were back in business.

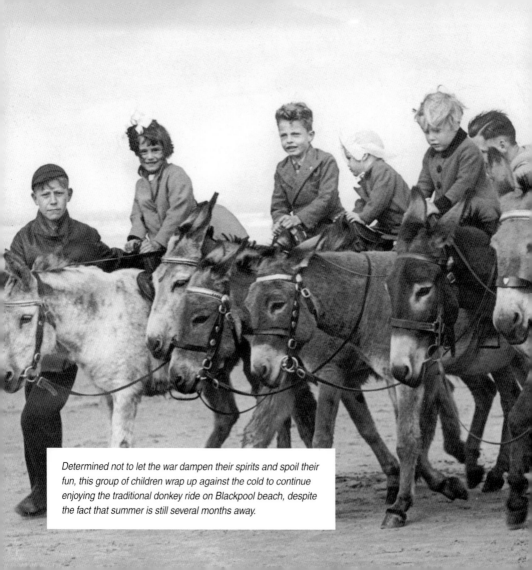

Determined not to let the war dampen their spirits and spoil their fun, this group of children wrap up against the cold to continue enjoying the traditional donkey ride on Blackpool beach, despite the fact that summer is still several months away.

By 1944 the country had grown accustomed to life played out against the backdrop of war. In fact, in some instances you could say people had become blasé, like this little boy, who clearly isn't bothered at all by the ominous warning sign washed up on the beach.

Above Children from London delight in the promise of a night or two under canvas in Elstree, away from the bombing raids. The Boy Scouts and Girl Guides did a valuable job of keeping children usefully distracted during the war and their camps provided city children with an opportunity to get away from it all.

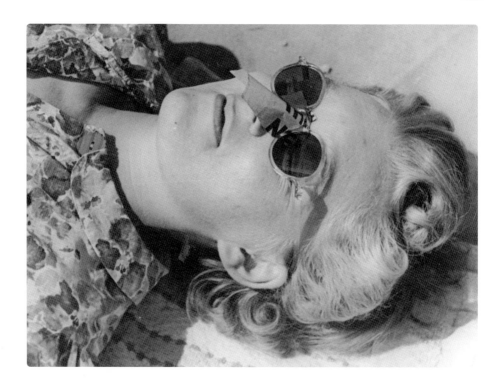

With victory in Europe just a week away, May Day 1945 brings people out for the traditional holiday festivities in hats and coats. Going to the beach wasn't so much about soaking up the sun as catching a lungful of bracing sea air and feeling that sense of collective liberation.

Above *It wasn't always easy to get away from the big city; sometimes you had to grab your holidays where you could. This nose-conscious sunbather has come to a holiday camp by the River Thames in Chertsey, Surrey, to top up her tan without getting her nose burnt.*

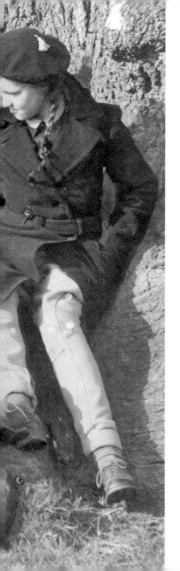

You pour, dear

Day one of the first spring of peacetime, 1946. A father, quite possibly celebrating being back in the bosom of his family after years of conflict, pours the dandelion and burdock as his girls hold out their cups during a picnic in the local park.

In the years immediately following the Second World War, more than four million British servicemen returned home. Many of them had been away for five or six years, during which time children they had never seen had been born and grown to school age. Others had grown from cuddly nippers into awkward teenagers. Many men felt like strangers in their own home and daily life proved a difficult challenge.

One way for reacquainted couples to alleviate the domestic tension was to go out together and recreate the wholesome pleasures of their own childhoods. And with more families owning their own cars, the British countryside was opening up to all.

After the war the good times began to roll again, as many of the restrictions on travel and recreation were lifted. These lucky people are enjoying life in the lap of luxury aboard an ocean-going cruiser without the threat of U-boats or mines.

Just over 30 miles from the coast of France, Ramsgate became a front line town during the Second World War and the beachside cafés gave way to fortifications and gun emplacements. As soon as the war was over, the crowds flocked back to spend their holidays in the popular seaside town.

Group activities were all the rage and Butlin's led the way, its famous Red Coats cajoling holidaymakers into taking part in mass entertainment and exercise classes with an almost Draconian zeal. This group of young girls are being put through their paces on the dance floor at Butlin's Camp in Filey.

It could almost be a parody of Hitler's Nuremberg Rally but it's actually a far more wholesome scene than that. These are holidaymakers at Butlin's Camp in Filey, North Yorkshire, taking part in a mass keep fit class. The Filey Camp had been requisitioned during the war and became RAF Hunmanby Moor.

Right The newfound confidence of the young British woman is captured for posterity by photographer Roy Kirby, who worked the beach front in Ramsgate after the Second World War. The cow looks positively pie-eyed as this bathing beauty poses for a never to be forgotten snapshot.

The sun shone brightly and the days slid lazily by. Long, languorous days just sitting on the beach in a deckchair, lulled by the gentle rhythm of the waves while the children amused themselves with buckets and spades making sandcastles. Peace at last.

A deckchair attendant in Eastbourne warms to his task. The deckchair, with its folding wooden frame full of comedy potential, had become a classic icon of the British seaside resort in the early part of the century and for postwar sunbathers it was the perfect accessory, especially on shingle beaches.

A tour guide keeps a busload of Swedish tourists amused during a sightseeing trip. As foreign travel increased after the war, Britain became a popular destination for overseas travellers, and the tourism industry began to open up to a whole new market.

Right *The beach was a fruitful place for making friends. It didn't matter where you came from, there were always bonds to be forged during the summer holidays. These two boys, aged 4 and 5, are from opposite ends of the country but have found common ground in the contents of a rock pool.*

Once on holiday, there was a strange reluctance to leave the beach, even when it poured with rain. If you didn't have a beach hut, you fashioned your own shelter, as these holidaymakers have done using deckchairs. Some hardy souls are still out defying the tide to come in, while a father plays cricket.

*Caravanners spruce up their holiday accommodation for the Easter break.
Caravanning had grown in popularity between the wars among those with
the means and the bohemian spirit; after the war, with more people able
to afford their own car, it enjoyed something of a boom.*

Turned Out Nice Again

The beauty pageant, the dance hall, the end-of-the-pier show and the ice cream van – the 1950s ushered in a new age of prosperity, levity and style that blew away the dark clouds of wartime and set the scene for Prime Minister Harold Macmillan to pronounce that much of the British population had 'never had it so good'.

More people were in work, so more people needed their holidays. The car was giving large numbers of them the freedom to explore parts of the country that hitherto had lain beyond their reach and they quickly began to find their way to the green spaces and beach fronts, some towing caravans, ready to embrace the great outdoors, others packing their dancing shoes, ready to embrace whoever accepted their hand on the dance floor.

The people in the holiday snaps from this era (now being taken on their own cameras) look somehow more knowing, more relaxed and comfortable with life, as if the shackles had been removed and they had been set free to draw the last drop of juice from their free time.

*Having buried their father up to his waist in the
Bournemouth sand without bothering to remove his
shirt, tie, sweater and jacket, two young girls pose for the
camera, which by the 1950s was being wielded by their
mother, not a professional beach photographer.*

It looks like a play-off in the final of the Women's World Gurning Championship, but this is what can happen when you go paddling in Southend at the wrong time of year. No matter how cold the sea might be, there was always an irresistible temptation to take your shoes off and have a paddle.

Out of the wind

'The sea, once it casts its spell, holds one in its net of wonder for ever,' wrote oceanologist Jacques Cousteau. There's something about connecting with the ocean that makes British holidaymakers very happy even on a freezing, wet and windy day. You see rows of them, lost in their own thoughts, sitting silently near the seafront and gazing out towards the horizon in a state of zen-like contemplation, warmed only by occasional sips of tea from their thermos flasks.

In 1956, Bognor Regis Council decided to run an experiment. With commendable forward thinking, they set up special perspex windscreens allowing visitors to watch the sea in comfort through a pane of glass, and waited for the crowds to roll up. But you know what? Watching the waves through a windscreen was like chewing gum with the wrapper on and eventually they took them down. People preferred to watch the waves the way they'd always done – without anything in between to interrupt the view.

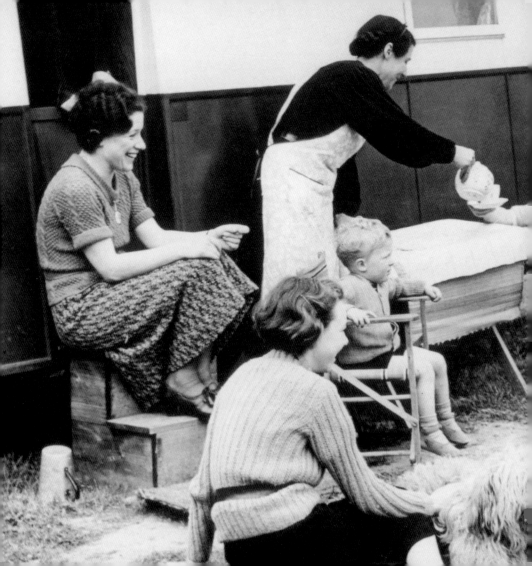

Youngsters could sleep under canvas if they wanted to, older campers were taking to the fields in caravans, towed there behind their new private motorcars. Camping and caravanning parks started springing up all over the country as groups like this took to the road in search of the freedom of the great outdoors.

An accordionist entertains a coachload of women on a day trip to Southend-on-Sea. Group outings were still the main source of escape for many Britons in the 1950s and a good old sing-song would help to pass the journey and add to the high spirits.

A prototype traffic jam in Dartmoor National Park. The downside of the boom in private car ownership was more cars on the road. Having driven hundreds of miles to visit Devon, you found that thousands of other car owners had had the same idea. The holiday traffic jam was born!

Austrian soprano Josette Adrienne gets a taste of the British seaside in the form of candy floss, sold to her on Brighton Pier. Having been invented in Europe, possibly as early as the 1500s, spun sugar was first marketed as 'fairy floss' and 'cotton candy' in the US, but became popular in Britain as candy floss.

Right *Here's a concept that works. The merry-go-round may have gained different means of propulsion, but to the rider the experience was unchanged from the early rides of the 19th century. For girls who couldn't afford their own pony, they provided all the thrills without the spills.*

Some grin, some shout out, some cover their ears, while others just look rather quizzical… the reactions of children to a Punch and Judy show in Margate speak volumes about their individual personalities, not to mention the universal popularity of this particular form of beachside entertainment.

Right *Nothing encapsulated the change in moral attitudes that took place after the Second World War more than the saucy seaside postcard – a genre of risqué cartoon humour that captured the holiday market for decades and became a design classic. This lady looks like she might have just recognized herself in one of the cartoons.*

Cold comfort

Nothing compares to the contrasting sensations of cold ice cream on a hot summer's day, as this toddler will testify – once she's finished eating. But there was a level of risk involved in eating your cornet on a sandy beach: drop it and all was lost! The sight of that ball of pure bliss lying at your feet, ruined by a covering of the dreaded gritty grains, could destroy your holiday fun – at least until the next day, when dad or mum would get you another.

You used to buy your ice creams from the beach café, but by the end of the 1950s the Mister Softee ice cream van had arrived in Britain, selling soft whipped ice cream that rivalled the old-style vanilla brick that was peddled by Wall's, usually accompanied by a rectangular cornet or a brittle wafer, seemingly designed to crumble just as you were bringing the ice cream to your lips. But now the dominion of the traditional vanilla cornet was about to be challenged by an exotic new menu of ice lollies.

Looking genuinely concerned that his cover might have been blown, a Punch and Judy puppeteer is caught on film as he surveys the lie of the land outside his show tent. You weren't supposed to see the man operating the puppets. They were real, living characters until the spell was broken.

Couples still in coats and hats embrace in a bout of ballroom dancing at the Pavilion Ballrooms in Rothesay, a popular resort with Glaswegians, on the Isle of Bute. Dancing was the great social outlet in the 1950s and the classic ballroom manoeuvres were familiar to all age groups.

Comedian Tommy Cooper entertains young holidaymakers on the beach in Great Yarmouth with his unique brand of madcap magicianship. Variety artists like Cooper pulled in big audiences to the end-of-the-pier theatres each summer, as British holidaymakers filled their days of leisure lapping up the entertainment.

When in holiday mood, the Brits could make an event of anything, and nowhere did it better than Butlin's. This holiday camper is being coy about his chances in the knobbly knees contest, while two Red Coats try to get a better look at his credentials.

An evangelist carries a stark warning about the divine retribution that awaits the crowds of holidaymakers in Brighton. 'You don't want God's love so prepare for God's wrath…' the sign proclaims. To some minds, the British seaside resort had become a den of vice.

Left *A young Jamaican boy looks after his family's luggage at Waterloo station in 1954. When you arrived in Britain from a foreign country, it could be an unnerving experience taking the train. That's because people didn't really speak much to each other, which could seem strange if you came from another culture.*

Right *A newlywed couple share a romantic moment on the beach in Jersey. By the 1950s, the popularity and accessibility of the seaside had one downside: trying to find your own space away from the crowds. The solution was to travel further afield. The days of overseas tourism were upon us.*

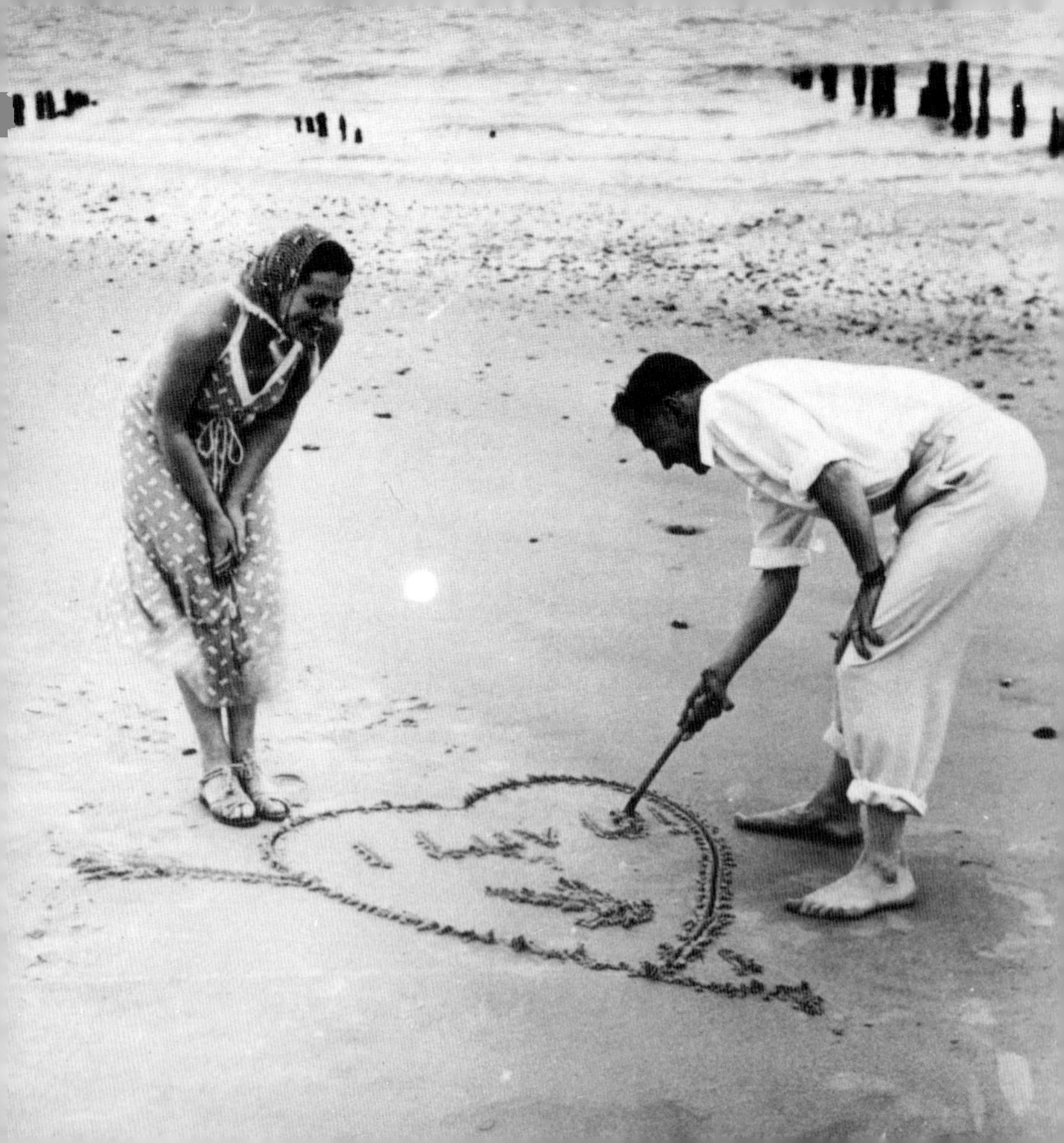

The Time of Our Lives

The 1960s saw the dawning of the modern holiday age:
air travel, car ferries, overseas resorts, bingo and children
seeking independence from their parents. The 1940s were
now far enough in the past for Europe to be
seen as a theatre of glamour, rather than a theatre of war and
travel companies were breaking new ground in opening up the
Continent to a wider section of the British population.

Most Brits still took their holidays at home and the
big resorts like Blackpool, Brighton, Great Yarmouth and
Eastbourne continued to do a roaring trade over the
summer months. There was an old-fashioned quality about
Britain's seaside towns, as if nostalgia was now their chief
commodity, but the allure of the coast still proved irresistible
to the nation's youth as they sought to exploit their newfound
freedom with wild bank holiday weekends away.

Not quite the Mr Universe contest, a motley line-up of wannabes flex their biceps at an amateur muscle man competition in the Lincolnshire seaside town of Mablethorpe. The two on the right are sporting the resigned expressions of men who know they haven't been putting in the hours.

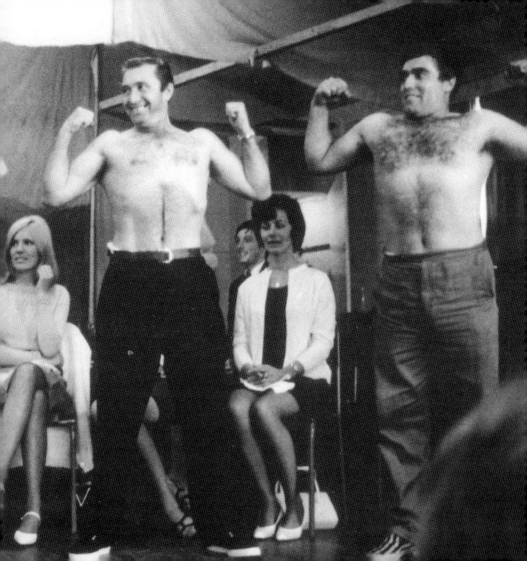

'Safety nets? Who needs 'em?' The latest in-beach entertainment in 1966 attracts a steady flow of participants, seemingly unconcerned by the danger of pinging off to one side and landing on the small boy with the spade, conscientiously digging in the foreground without any regard for his own safety.

Above The regular morning show in the Redoubt Music Gardens, Eastbourne, gets the day off to a flying start for these children and their parents. Children's entertainment would be laid on every day throughout the holiday season and there would always be an enthusiastic audience.

Brits abroad

The 1950s had seen the beginning of the boom in holidays abroad, with a million Britons seeking sunnier climes in 1950. Four years later a change in civil aviation law was exploited by package tour operators to enable them to take tourists abroad on charter planes. A nation still getting used to having its own private transport was now being given the freedom of the skies. A fortnight in Skegness was no longer exotic enough; now we wanted guaranteed sunshine, tanned skin and sangria!

It was the British thirst for beach holidays that created the seaside resort, not just in Britain but all over the world. Once the floodgates had been opened there was no going back. By the 1960s small fishing villages like Benidorm were being transformed into swarming resorts (as pictured), typified by high-rise hotels, tuxedoed Spanish waiters and lobster red British holidaymakers.

While the young generation brought their youthful zeal and hunger for the new to holiday season, the elderly – veterans of two world wars – found their own pleasures in a vacant deckchair, watching it all unfold. This group of old friends are sharing a picnic on Brighton beach.

Left *Slogger Hoad, aka 'The Winkle King of Hastings', models the suit and cap he made by sewing together winkle shells. The outfit took him six months to make and used 9,626 shells, but you have to agree it was well worth the effort.*

Right *An elderly lady sits on the verandah of her neatly appointed beach hut in Scarborough. Before the war the beach hut had replaced the bathing tent as a place to don your costume in privacy and now proliferated around Britain's coastal towns, where they served as a place to dry off, have tea and shelter from the weather.*

It takes two

A lone couple trip the light fantastic in one of Britain's remaining dance halls in Morecambe. On stage, the big band of years gone by has been whittled down to just a keyboard and drums.

Ballroom dancing went into decline in the 1960s. The kids were into rock'n'roll and rejected the dance steps of their parents' generation in favour of a more individual style of movement. Consequently, the dance hall became less of a social hub and its role as a major draw for the holiday crowds died out.

In its place came the bingo hall. The generation who had danced in the 1940s and 50s now preferred the more sedentary lottery game and the chance to win a cuddly toy for their grandchild. Bingo became very popular in the 1960s and by the end of the decade was as much a part of the British seaside town as deckchairs, funfairs and sticks of rock.

On a bright, sunny day in Brighton, young love flourishes on the Palace Pier while, across the divide, men whose courting days are long since gone while away the lonely hours with a smoke and a sit down in the sunshine.

A gang of Mods huddle together by a jellied eel stand in Clacton, on a fateful Whitsun weekend in 1964 when Mods and Rockers ran riot in the town. Youth culture had developed a violent rebellious side, which was repeatedly played out in the seaside towns of south-east England.

Paul McCartney attracts a gaggle of surprisingly grown-up-looking autograph-hunters while making a surprise appearance on Newquay beach during the filming of The Beatles' film The Magical Mystery Tour. *The film, mostly conceived by McCartney, was a cornucopia of British eccentricities, no doubt inspired in part by the holiday crowd.*

A man wearing a child's cowboy hat cuddles his fellow marshal as he sleeps in the sun on the beach at Eastbourne. Meanwhile, behind them, it's bikinis all the way in the women's beach fashion stakes, but still shirts and hats for the older generation on the prom.

Discovering the Continent

A family take sustenance on the bonnet of their car as they wait in the queue for the Newhaven–Dieppe ferry. The first cross-Channel car ferries had come into operation before the Second World War but the process had been slow and cumbersome, requiring each car to be loaded by crane. By the 1960s the drive-on car ferry, plus the proliferation of privately owned cars, was adding an exciting new dimension to the menu of holiday options.

Middle-class Brits were now able to drive from their door to the fields and beaches of France, Belgium, Germany and beyond. Words like 'gîte', 'Strudel', 'camembert' and 'duty-free' entered the vocabulary. And, of course, the dreaded 'breakdown'. Any car that travelled further than 100 miles was likely to conk out at some point in the journey, requiring Dad to find a local mechanic and negotiate in pidgin French, while Mum tried to keep the children amused with a hot chocolate at the local café.

British holidaymakers flying abroad soon discovered one thing: airline schedules were not set in stone. Flights could be interrupted by all sorts of weather conditions, including snow or hurricane-strength winds, but the words passengers came to dread most were 'strike by air-traffic control'. Industrial action could ground planes across Europe and lead to long nights in the passenger lounge.

Three British models soak up the sun on the Côte d'Azur. The South of France was the lap of luxury – the playground of film stars like Brigitte Bardot – but it was becoming increasingly accessible for British holidaymakers. Once you had tasted that hot sun and warm water, it was hard to go back to Bridlington.

A stewardess helps a group of well-heeled travellers aboard a coach at Gatwick Airport as they prepare to jet off to the Continent. Flying was still an expensive way of going on holiday, with those who could afford it being dubbed the 'Jet Set'.

Two backpackers looking fresh and clean prepare to take their first steps on the Hippie Trail. From the mid-1960s, the Trail took British travellers through Europe and beyond to the mystical wonders of Pakistan, India and Nepal. By the time they came back, the combed hair and pristine white clothes were no more.

A bank holiday weekend brings the crowds flocking to Blackpool beach to indulge in the time-honoured pastimes of building sandcastles, riding donkeys, paddling in the sea and warming your hands around a hot cup of Oxo. The simple traditions were still going strong.

Above As another holiday season comes to an end, two men in hats from the South Wales resort of Barry Island return the 'try your weight' machine to the shed for winter storage. The shutters come down, windows are boarded up and the British seaside town goes into hibernation for another year.

It's 1961 and a group of honeymooners have arranged themselves into a heart shape on a Jersey beach. In the 1950s, Jersey became known as 'the honeymoon island' and the place was packed out with newlyweds. There were so many that hotels started bolting single beds together to accommodate them. Back then, the British government offered tax breaks if you got married before 6 April. You could claim Married Man's Allowance for the whole tax year, which often paid for your honeymoon. Those were the days.

Picture Credits
All photographs supplied by Getty Images.